This book belongs to

_____

Published by arrangement with Lion Publishing.
Newfield Publications and Newfield Publications and design
are federally registered trademarks of Newfield Publications, Inc..

Based on the *Lion Story Bible* series originally published by Lion Publishing
20 Lincoln Ave.
Elgin, IL 60120

Library of Congress Cataloging–In–Publication Data

Frank, Penny.
    David and Goliath / story by Penny Frank; illustrated by Tony
Morris; additional material by Daniel Burow.
      p. cm. — (Children's story Bible.)
    Summary: Retells the Biblical story of David, the shepherd boy, who
fought and killed the giant Goliath. Includes an introduction for parents
and a brief section with background information.
    ISBN 0–7459–2606–1
    1. David, King of Israel—Juvenile literature. 2. Goliath (Biblical giant)—
Juvenile literature. 3. Bible stories, English—O.T. Samuel, 1st. [1. David,
King of Israel. 2. Goliath (Biblical giant) 3. Bible stories—O.T.] I. Morris,
Tony, ill. II. Burow, Daniel R. III. Title IV. Series: Frank, Penny.
Children's story Bible.
BS580.D3F68 1992
222'.4309505—dc20   92–20481

Printed in the United States of America

David and Goliath

Story by Penny Frank
Illustrated by Tony Morris

Additional material by Daniel Burow

Design: Melanie Lawson

NEWFIELD PUBLICATIONS
Shelton, Connecticut

The Bible tells us how God chose the Israelites to be his special people. God promised to love and care for them always.

Sometimes the Israelites found that promise hard to believe. When a soldier as big as a giant came after them, they did not believe God could take care of them.

David believed God's promise and quietly picked up some smooth stones. The giant Goliath just laughed.

You can find the story of David and Goliath in your own Bible, in the first book of Samuel, chapter 17.

David was the youngest of eight sons.
His father was a shepherd called Jesse.
    When David was growing up, the
prophet Samuel visited Jesse's family. He
told them that, when King Saul died,
David would be the next king of Israel.

God had especially chosen him, so
David knew that God was with him in a
special way.

David worked hard.

'God has to teach me to be a really
good shepherd before he can make me a
good king,' he said.

4

David played the harp and sang his own
songs about God. King Saul sometimes
asked David to go to the palace and sing
for him. When the king was in a bad
mood, David's songs made him feel
better.

David's brothers were soldiers. They fought in King Saul's army. They were often away from home for a long time.

Their father was pleased that David was at home to keep him company. He was an old man and David helped him look after the sheep.

David often spent days and nights out on the hills. He had to take the sheep to places where there was grass and water.

There were lions, wild bears and wolves living in the hills. David was sometimes afraid.

He had to fight off the wild animals to keep the lambs and sheep safe.

One day when David came back from
the hills, his father said, 'You can leave
the sheep for one of the men to look
after. I want you to go to visit your
brothers. Take them some good food and
bring me back news of them.'

So David packed some food and set off on the journey.

It was a long way, but David knew the hills very well.

At last he found his brothers with the Israelite army. They looked really frightened.

'What's the matter?' David asked.

They pointed to the hill across the valley. 'Over there, with the Philistine soldiers, is the giant Goliath,' they said 'He wants one of us to fight him.'

'Well, why don't you?' asked David.
'You are the army of the living God. You will win.'

'If you're so brave, then come and tell the king you'll go,' sneered the brothers.

They were very surprised when David did just as they said. He told the king that he would go to fight Goliath, and that God would fight for him.

'You must have my helmet and sword,' said King Saul.

But everything was so heavy that David could not stand up.

'I can't wear this,' David said, 'I'll just take the sling and stones I use when I am a shepherd.'

He took his sling and carefully chose five smooth stones from beside the stream.

When Goliath saw David walking across the valley towards him, he laughed so loudly that the Israelites had to cover up their ears.

Goliath had a sword and a shield.

But when he saw that David had brought only stones and a sling, he was angry.

'Do you think you are only fighting to keep your sheep safe?' he jeered.

But David knew how to fight with
stones. He took out his sling as he
walked. He fitted a stone into it.

When he was close to Goliath he
shouted, 'I come against you in the
name of the living God!'

David swung the sling around and around above his head. When he let go, the stone flew out and hit Goliath on his forehead. It was just the one place where he could be hurt.

The stone killed Goliath.

David drew the giant's own sword and cut off his head.

When the Philistines saw that Goliath was dead, they ran away.

The Israelites cheered when they saw what David had done to Goliath. They ran after the Philistines, driving them out of their land.

All the Israelites heard that David had won the battle. They knew the Philistines had run away.

They danced in the streets and sang songs about David, the brave shepherd.

King Saul grew jealous because everyone was talking about David.

David had learned to trust God when he
was a shepherd. Now he had killed a
giant because he knew that the God of
Israel was the living God, who helps his
people.

David would know how to trust God
when he became king.

Do You Know?

David's people lived in the hills. But they also wanted land near the sea. The Philistines built ships and lived by the sea. They wanted land in the hills. The two groups fought over each other's land.

The Philistines were dangerous because they had iron weapons. The Israelites didn't have furnaces and tools to make such weapons.

When David reached his brothers, the armies weren't fighting. They were on two hills. To attack, the armies would have to climb up their enemy's hill. It is hard to fight while climbing a hill. So both armies stayed where they were.

The tallest Philistine soldier was Goliath. The Bible says he was about 9 feet tall. Goliath suggested that the strongest person in each army fight. Then only one person would get killed instead of many.

A sling was a piece of leather shepherds used to throw stones. They practiced with their slings so they could scare away wild animals that tried to hurt their sheep.

NOTE TO PARENTS

The story of David and Goliath comes from one of the Old Testament history books: 1 Samuel, chapter 17. It is drawn from the early life of David, who went on to become the greatest king Israel ever had.

At the time of the story, Israel was beginning to experiment with the idea of a monarchy. Saul was Israel's first king. He was a capable military leader; but, according to the Bible, he disobeyed the Lord on several occasions. As a consequence, God sent the prophet Samuel to Bethlehem to find and anoint David as the next king.

David was still quite young and totally unknown. He would continue to live in the shadow of King Saul for some years. But as Saul's personal court musician and as a captain in Saul's army, David learned about the life of a king, and he learned how to lead and rule.

The great threat that Saul and Israel faced at the time came from the Philistines. Like the Israelites, the Philistines were relative newcomers to the land. As they expanded inland from the sea, they came into conflict with the Israelites.

The story of David defeating Goliath tells how David rose to fame in Israel and how he became a captain in Saul's army. The story does more. It declares that what makes a person or people great is not size or technology but trust in the Lord.